The Kids Laugh Challenge

Would You Rather?

Easter Edition

Funny Scenarios, Wacky Choices and Hilarious Situations for Kids and Family

With Fun Illustrations

RIDDLELAND

Table of Contents

Riddleland Bonus Book

Join our **Facebook Group** at **Riddleland for Kids** to get daily jokes and riddles.

http://pixelfy.me/riddlelandbonus

Thank you for buying this book. We would like to share a special bonus as a token of appreciation. It is a collection of 50 original jokes, riddles, and two super funny stories.

Introduction

"Egg hunts are proof that your children can find things when they really want." ~ **Unknown**

We would like to personally thank you for purchasing this book. ***Would You Rather? Easter Edition*** is a collection of the funniest scenarios, wacky choices, and hilarious situations for kids and adults to choose from.

These questions are an excellent way to get a conversation started in a fun and exciting way. Also, by asking "Why?" after a "Would you rather" question, you may find interesting answers and learn a lot about a person.

We wrote this book because we want children to be encouraged to read more, think, and grow. As parents, we know that when children play games and learn, they are being educated while having so much fun that they don't even realize they're learning and developing valuable life skills. 'Would you Rather …' is one of our favorite games to play as a family. Some of the 'would you rather …' scenarios have had us in fits of giggles, others have generated reactions such as: "Eeeeeeuuugh, that's gross!" and yet others still really make us think and reflect and consider our decisions.

Besides having fun, playing the game also has other benefits such as:

- **Communication** – This game helps children to interact, read aloud, and listen to others. It's a great way to connect. It's a fun way for parents to get their children interacting with them without a formal, awkward conversation. The game can also help to get to know someone better and learn about their likes, dislikes, and values.

- **Builds Confidence** - Children get used to pronouncing vocabulary, asking questions and it helps to deal with shyness.

- **Develops Critical Thinking** – It helps children to defend and justify the rationale for their choices and can generate discussions and debates. Parents playing this game with young children can give them prompting questions about their answers to help them reach logical and sensible decisions.

- **Improves Vocabulary** – Children will be introduced to new words in the questions, and the context of them will help them remember them because the game is fun.

- **Encourages Equality and Diversity** – Considering other people's answers, even if they differ from your own, is important for respect, equality, diversity, tolerance, acceptance, and inclusivity. Some questions may get children to think about options available to them, that don't fall into gendered stereotypes, i.e., careers or activities that challenge the norm.

Welcome to The Kids Laugh Challenge
Would You Rather?
Easter Edition

How do you play?

At least two players are needed to play this game. Face your opponent and decide who is **Easter Bunny 1** and **Easter Bunny 2**. If you have 3 or 4 players, you can decide which players belong to **Easter Bunny Group 1** and **Easter Bunny Group 2**. The goal of the game is to score points by making the other players laugh. The first player to a score of 10 points is the **Champion**.

What are the rules?

Easter Bunny 1 starts first. Read the questions aloud and choose an answer. The same player will then explain why they chose the answer in the silliest and wackiest way possible. If the reason makes Easter Bunny 2 laugh, then Easter Bunny 1 scores a funny point. Take turns going back and forth and write down the score.

How do you get started?

Flip a coin. The Easter Bunny that guesses it correctly starts first.

Bonus Tip: Making funny voices, silly dance moves or wacky facial expression will make your opponent laugh!

Most importantly: Remember to have fun and enjoy the game!

 # Would You Rather...

Roll around in a field of daisies and come out smelling like a rose OR roll around in a field of tulips and come out smelling like a daisy?

Go to school on Easter but get a bunch of candy all day long OR get Easter off from school but not get any candy all day long?

Would You Rather...

Go to school dressed as a tie-dyed Easter bunny OR walk around school all day with a rotten egg cracked on top of your head?

Sleep sitting on a nest of fragile duck eggs that need to be kept warm OR spend an afternoon picking up little rabbit poos from all over your yard?

Would You Rather...

Walk around for a day with a shoe full of speckled jellybeans OR wear shoes made from puffy marshmallow bunny rabbits?

Be trapped for one day inside a giant milk chocolate Easter bunny OR get a giant milk chocolate Easter bunny in your Easter basket with both of its ears bitten off?

Would You Rather...

Be a vegetarian and only eat things like carrots and lettuce just like the Easter Bunny OR be addicted to sugar and only eat sugar cookies like Santa Claus?

Eat all your food by getting it out of plastic Easter eggs OR eat food (not Easter eggs) that is dyed pastel colors?

Would You Rather...

Wake up covered in blue speckles all over your body like a robin's egg OR wake up to find yourself sleeping in a robin's nest up in a tree and have no idea how you got there?

Peck at the ground and eat wriggly slimy worms OR lay a random egg at least once a week every week?

Would You Rather...

Have Easter basket grass stuck in between your toes OR have a bunch of chick feathers stuck in your hair that you just can't get out?

Find your Easter basket in a warm oven so that all your chocolate yummies have melted OR find your Easter basket in the freezer so that all the candy is rock hard?

 Would You Rather...

Wear the big awkward feet of an Easter Bunny costume OR wear a big floppy bunny ear headband to school for a week?

Go on an Easter egg hunt while blindfolded and unable to see a thing OR go on an Easter egg hunt and have your hands tied behind your back the whole time?

 # Would You Rather...

Have the webbed feet of a duckling that don't fit into any shoes but help you to be an awesome swimmer OR make the quacking sound of a duck every time you open your mouth?

Walk across a playground covered with broken Easter eggshells OR play around in a sandbox filled with jellybeans instead of sand?

Would You Rather...

Have crazy green Easter basket grass growing out of your head instead of hair OR wear pants made from woven Easter basket material?

Sleep in an Easter basket covered with grass instead of covered by a blanket in your bed OR sleep cozy and warm inside an egg waiting to hatch?

 # Would You Rather...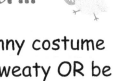

Wear a thick fluffy Easter Bunny costume for a whole day and get super sweaty OR be picked up from school one day by your mom dressed up in an Easter Bunny costume?

Make homemade bunny-shaped cinnamon rolls with raisins for eyes OR try to scramble eggs in the shape of little chicks for breakfast?

 # Would You Rather...

Have bunny whiskers that constantly tickle your face OR a pink bunny nose that randomly twitches throughout the day?

See a flurry of fluffy feathers floating around your bedroom every time you walk into it OR hear phantom chirping chick noises every night as you lay down to go to sleep?

Would You Rather...

Find random clumps of bunny fur in your clothes every day OR find muddy little bunny paw prints all over your house every day?

Go to school with a cute and fluffy little yellow chick stuffed in your pants pocket OR try to keep the cute and fluffy little yellow chick stuffed into your desk so no one sees it all day?

Would You Rather...

Go to school transformed into a big chocolate Easter bunny OR be the only person at your school who is not a big chocolate Easter bunny?

Have an egg and spoon race where you run with a raw egg balanced on a spoon OR have an egg toss contest where you see who can catch a raw egg from the farthest distance without it breaking?

Would You Rather...

Imagine your teacher has turned into a big chocolate bunny every time you look at him or her OR be sitting in a desk made entirely out of chocolate?

Spend spring break building and hanging out in the coolest backyard treehouse in your own backyard OR going to a week-long camp of your choice?

 # Would You Rather...

Take a painting class where you try to paint the Easter Bunny carrying a basket of Easter eggs OR try to make a homemade Easter Bunny using a bunch of cotton balls, glue, and a carrot?

Skip going trick-or-treating one year on Halloween and get no candy OR get stiffed out of your Easter basket goodies (no candy) by the Easter Bunny?

Would You Rather...

Eat only beautifully dyed hard-boiled eggs for a week after Easter OR eat nothing but salty pink Easter ham for the week after Easter?

Be forced to eat every single piece of Easter candy in your basket on Easter Sunday OR only be able to eat one piece every day until it is all gone?

Would You Rather...

Have 100 little chocolate Easter bunnies OR have one big chocolate Easter bunny that is as tall as you are?

Hunt for Easter eggs in the snow and the eggs are all buried under big piles of snowflakes OR hunt for Easter eggs after a nice spring rain shower has put all the eggs into little mud puddles?

Would You Rather...

Weave your own Easter basket out
banana peels OR out of dried corn husks
from autumn?

Eat a delicious homemade Easter dinner
with all your favorite holiday foods OR go
to a restaurant's Easter buffet and have a
choice of any kind of food you can imagine,
not necessarily your favorites and not
necessarily fresh?

 # Would You Rather...

Get a piece of Easter basket grass in your mouth while eating a chocolate egg OR get a piece of your own hair in your mouth?

Go Easter egg hunting at night searching for glow-in-the-dark eggs OR go Easter egg hunting after a rainstorm has washed away most of the eggs' dye?

 # Would You Rather...

Eat only foods made from chocolate or covered in chocolate for the rest of your life OR never be able to eat chocolate again?

Pull the best April Fool's Day prank on your sibling but get in trouble with your parents OR spend a long time putting together the best April Fool's Day prank and then it spectacularly backfires?

Would You Rather...

Be required to take a picture of every single Easter egg you find in a hunt OR put them all in a basket and carry them around with you?

Be followed to school every day by an orderly little line of fluffy yellow chicks chirping merrily OR a hippity hoppity line of little bunnies with cute floppy ears?

Would You Rather...

Have an Easter lily in your bedroom that looks beautiful but smells bad OR have one that smells good but makes you sneeze?

Collect enough honey from beehives to fill up a big jar OR snip fresh cut flowers from the garden while being chased by bees who want to collect pollen from your flowers?

Would You Rather...

Grow a cute little cotton ball tail like a bunny rabbit OR lose all but your two front teeth which grow larger and stick out of your mouth like a little bunny rabbit?

Wake up to see the ground covered with a blanket of fresh new snow on the first day of spring OR be woken up to a rumbly downpouring thunderstorm?

Would You Rather...

Work at a chocolate factory surrounded by yummy chocolate goodies and smells but not be able to eat chocolate OR work at a farm supervising the chicken coops and collecting eggs from the hens every day?

Stuff twenty marshmallow chicks into your mouth OR sneeze chocolate milk out of your nose?

Would You Rather...

Find twenty chocolate Easter eggs that are kind of old and tasteless OR one small chocolate Easter egg that tastes absolutely perfect?

Dye two dozen Easter eggs and only have one of those eggs look the way that you want OR only get to dye one egg and take your chances that it looks the way that you want?

Would You Rather...

Wear a perfume or cologne that smells like your favorite flower OR one that smells like your favorite candy bar?

Try to guess how many jellybeans are in a jar and the closest guess wins the whole jar OR eat a bunch of funky flavored jellybeans (like tomato soup) blindfolded and try to guess the flavor?

Would You Rather...

Search through a very large hen house full of smelly chickens to find the one that lays golden eggs OR dig into the garbage dumpster every day because someone throws away a fully wrapped king-sized candy bar?

Work at a pet store cleaning out the rabbit cages OR scrubbing out the insides of the fish tanks?

 # Would You Rather...

Decorate your bedroom for Easter by gluing a bunch of minty green Easter basket grass on the walls OR by hanging a bunch of real Easter eggs from the ceiling with string and staples?

Play a game of Pin the Cotton Ball (tail) on the Bunny OR go bowling using an Easter egg instead of a bowling ball?

Would You Rather...

Sit on a big oval Easter egg instead of a chair at your desk OR play in a sandbox filled with jellybeans at recess?

Get an Easter basket filled with real grass from your lawn mower bag OR one full of plain raw white eggs from the carton in your refrigerator?

Would You Rather...

Perform the chicken dance in front
of the whole school while dressed in
a feathered chicken costume OR the
bunny hop while dressed in a giant
rabbit costume?

Get an Easter basket full of hard and
chewy fruit flavored jellybeans OR get
an Easter basket full of soft and sugary
licorice-only jellybeans?

37

 Would You Rather...

Eat a special Easter meal of two thick slices of salty ham with one piece of buttered bread sandwiched in between OR eat a sandwich made from two slices of buttered bread with a bunch of jellybeans stuck in between?

Paint Easter eggs with leaves from the trees outside OR by using pieces of grass from your yard?

 # Would You Rather...

Walk to school by hopping like a bunny OR
by waddling the whole way like a duck?

Spend one Easter filling in for the Easter
Bunny and spending your whole night before
Easter sneaking around hiding Easter baskets
for kids OR spend all day on Easter looking
for your Easter basket and not being able
to find it?

 # Would You Rather...

Have a body that is like a big oval pastel-colored plastic Easter egg OR hair that is green and crazy like a big handful of Easter basket grass?

OH MY! MY HAIR LOOKS LIKE A GREEN EASTER BASKET GRASS.

Crack every single one of your Easter eggs as you're dying them OR open up a dozen raw eggs and find half of them are cracked before you can even dye them?

Would You Rather...

Try to make a polka dot dyed Easter egg by using a white crayon to draw perfect little circles OR try to make a striped dyed Easter egg by drawing perfectly straight lines all around your egg?

Play a game of hopscotch with a very bouncy rabbit OR double Dutch jump rope with two energetic rabbits?

 Would You Rather...

Accidentally dye a carton full of eggs that have not yet been hard boiled OR find a smelly boiled Easter egg in June that no one found before?

Play dodgeball in gym class using a bunch of real eggs that explode yolks at you when you get hit OR a bunch of plastic eggs that are filled with jellybeans and pop open showering you with jellybeans?

Would You Rather...

Have a pet bunny rabbit that poops chocolate chips OR chocolate covered raisins?

Go on an Easter egg hunt where all the eggs are camouflaged to their surroundings (eggs in the grass are green, etc.) OR go on an Easter egg hunt where all the eggs are rotten, smelly, easy to find, and not at all fun?

 Would You Rather...

Grow beautiful and fragrant flowers in your garden OR grow delicious and nutritious vegetables in your garden this spring?

Pay someone to hunt for your Easter basket by giving them one-fourth of your candy out of the basket OR by giving them the money that the tooth fairy leaves you for your next four lost teeth?

 # Would You Rather...

Fall on the ground and get mud plus grass stains all over the knees of your pants OR fall on the ice and get holes in both knees of your pants?

Spend all night crouched under the couch in your living room trying to catch the Easter Bunny OR spend all night huddled in the bottom of your chimney waiting for Santa to slide down?

Would You Rather...

Get licorice-flavored jellybeans OR coconut-flavored jellybeans if your Easter basket could only be filled with one flavor?

Go out for recess on a spring day after it's just rained, and all of the playground equipment is wet OR go out for recess on a cold spring day where everything is coated with a layer of ice?

Would You Rather...

Listen to a story about how your Grandma or Grandpa spent Easter when they were a kid OR how your mom or dad spent Easter when they were a kid?

Carry a backpack full of unboiled Easter eggs OR a backpack full of foil-wrapped chocolate Easter eggs to school on a warm day?

Would You Rather...

Drive around in a car that looks like a giant Easter egg OR in a car that looks like a giant Easter basket?

Be in Haux, France, on Easter Monday and eat part of an omelet that uses over 4,500 eggs and feeds over 1,000 people OR eat an omelet for breakfast at home every single day for a year?

Would You Rather...

Break up a squawking fight between a pair of birds in a tree outside your bedroom window OR break up a chicken fight that breaks out in a hen house?

March down your street dressed in your fanciest clothes for your neighborhood's Easter Parade on Easter morning OR get caught outside searching for Easter eggs in your pajamas?

Would You Rather...

Get a very long piece of green Easter basket grass wrapped around your pinkie toe inside of your sock OR a very clingy piece of green Easter basket grass that you just can't shake off your fingers?

Spill a mug full of Easter egg dye on your favorite shirt OR spill a mug of Easter egg dye all over your hands leaving them stained for days?

Would You Rather...

Color Easter eggs using a bunch of broken crayon pieces OR a bunch of dried out markers?

Wake up one morning to find a bunch of Easter basket grass in your belly button with a robin nesting in the middle of it OR wake up one morning in the tree outside your window sitting on a nest of robin's eggs?

Would You Rather...

Put on an Easter Bunny suit after someone got really hot and sweaty in it OR get the head part of the Easter Bunny costume stuck on your face for an hour after you should be done wearing it?

Roll head over heels like a tucked-in hedgehog down a grassy green hill OR doggy paddle your way across a duck pond?

Would You Rather...

Pluck the petals off a bundle of eight daisies, one by one, OR count every piece of Easter basket grass in your basket?

Go to the White House and participate in the official Easter egg roll with other kids OR go to a park and take part in an Easter egg hunt with other kids?

 # Would You Rather...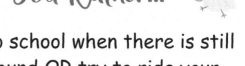

Ride your bike to school when there is still snow on the ground OR try to ride your skateboard to school on an icy day?

Dye all your Easter eggs the same color, whichever color you choose OR have to dye all of your Easter eggs the same color, but one that someone else chooses for you?

Would You Rather...

Get an Easter basket full of 500 pennies OR one plastic Easter egg with a $5 bill in it?

Go to Corfu, Greece, the day before Easter when lots of people stand on their balconies and literally throw pots out onto the street OR stand by yourself on your porch or deck and throw pots out onto your yard?

 Would You Rather...

Eat a cheese Easter egg instead of a chocolate one OR eat a purely dark chocolate Easter egg?

Wake up super early on Easter morning to go look for your Easter basket and realize it's only Saturday OR oversleep on Easter morning and find your little brother or sister has found your basket and eaten a bunch of the candy?

Would You Rather...

Listen to the sound of the rain falling on your roof but feel like it's falling on your head OR the sound of a strong wind blowing against your wall but feel like it's blowing your hair?

Plant a garden filled entirely with your favorite flower OR a garden with tons of different colored and scented flowers?

 # Would You Rather...

Feel the warm sun on your face after a long cold winter while wearing a tank top OR feel the gentle breeze against your skin while wearing a pair of shorty shorts?

Eat a donut covered from top to bottom with coconut flakes OR eat a glazed donut that has raisins all over the inside of it?

Would You Rather...

Craft a birdhouse out of a smelly old milk carton OR out of a sticky old soda bottle?

Make a Ukrainian Easter egg by poking holes in both ends of a raw egg with a needle and blowing out the yolk and then spending hours decorating an intricate design on the egg OR spend hours picking up, by hand, every single piece of Easter basket grass that you accidently dumped on your living room floor?

59

 Would You Rather...

Draw a self-portrait in chalk outside on a sidewalk OR fingerpaint a self-portrait on paper using melted Easter egg chocolate?

Have laser vision while on an Easter egg hunt so you can see through any obstacle the eggs are hidden in or behind OR have really long stretchy arms that can reach out and snatch eggs that you see far away?

Would You Rather...

Get stuck going birdwatching with your grandparents and end up getting bird poop on your sleeve OR get your finger bit by a duck while trying to feed it some breadcrumbs?

Go on an Easter Egg hunt in a field full of brightly colored flowers OR in a huge mansion with fifty different rooms?

Would You Rather...

Read your favorite springtime book inside a cool hollowed-out log near your house OR read your favorite Easter book after climbing up into a cozy tree?

Mow the growing tall green grass in your yard OR shovel a few inches of snow from your driveway and sidewalks on the first day of spring?

Would You Rather...

Be the last one to jump in the pool OR the first person to find a golden egg in an Easter egg hunt?

Wake up before the sun on Easter morning to search for your Easter basket but not be able to see anything because of all the eye boogers in your eyes OR be so tired that you sleep the entire day of Easter away and receive no candy?

Would You Rather...

Try to build a rock sculpture with a bunch of round egg-shaped rocks that keep toppling over OR try to see through a pair of sunglasses with dirty fingerprints all over them?

Build a treehouse that is protected from invasion by birds and critters OR one that is protected from invasion by your siblings and parents?

Would You Rather...

Have one of the straps of your backpack totally rip off on your way to school scattering Easter candy on the floor OR have one of your shoelaces bust in half while you're on your way home from school meaning it takes you longer and a sibling will eat some of your Easter candy?

File your fingernails down on the bark of a tree OR brush your teeth by gnawing on a tree twig?

 # Would You Rather...

Dye your Easter eggs using natural foods like spinach juice and boiled beets OR by crushing flower petals and smearing them all over the boiled eggs?

Spend Easter with your family doing fun family activities on Easter OR spend Easter with friends having Easter Egg hunts and eating candy together?

Would You Rather...

Braid friendship bracelets out of Easter basket grass OR twist a bunch of foil chocolate egg wrappers into friendship necklaces?

Sleep curled up in the center of a very large flower that tucks you into its petals at night OR sleep next to a wooly lamb who shares her woolen warmth with you like a blanket?

Would You Rather...

Hear the sound of a bee buzzing by your ear all day long OR the sound of a seashell in your ear while you're trying to fall asleep?

Dye your Easter eggs by holding them in your mouth and dunking your face into a cup of dye OR dye your Easter eggs by holding them with your fingers and dunking them into a cup of dye?

Would You Rather...

Find money from another country in your Easter basket OR find candies you don't recognize from other countries in your Easter basket?

Be responsible for the Easter Bunny tripping over a mess in your house and twisting his ankle OR be responsible for Santa Claus breaking off a tooth on a too-hard sugar cookie?

Would You Rather...

Find a chocolate Easter bunny with your face on it, in your Easter basket OR a bunch of marshmallow chicks with your brother or sister's face on them?

Spend spring break doing a deep spring clean of your bedroom OR spend spring break doing a deep dive into spring yard chores with your parents?

Would You Rather...

Only taste peppermint toothpaste flavor any time you eat anything chocolate OR use toothpaste that tastes like your least favorite flavor of jellybeans?

Build a fort out of pillows and blankets in the springtime with nothing to hook them together OR try to build a hideout using branches that have no leaves because it's winter?

Would You Rather...

Catch sight of the Easter bunny running
away from your house and see that he
wasn't wearing any clothes OR watch
a chicken laying an egg?

Paint ugly rocks with sayings of kindness
to hide for others to find OR paint cracked
eggs to hide on the playground for your
friends to find?

Would You Rather...

Find a bunch of muddy footprints all over your bedroom floor OR find blobs of green jello all over your bedroom floor?

Be dragged around to a bunch of spring garage sales early on a Saturday morning OR wake up early on a Saturday morning to drag trash bags out of the house after spring cleaning?

Would You Rather...

Work on a computer with a keyboard made from chocolate OR use a computer mouse made from chocolate?

Wake up on Easter morning only to find that your siblings put all their coconut jellybeans into your basket OR that someone has bit one ear off every chocolate Easter bunny in your basket?

Would You Rather...

Have a family of chicks nesting underneath your bed OR a family of rabbits nesting in the clothes in your closet?

Paint a masterpiece using brushes and different thicknesses of mud from your yard OR create a mosaic (pieced together art) by gluing pieces of colored eggshells onto a sheet of paper?

 # Would You Rather...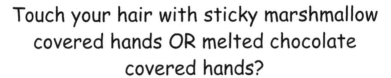

Touch your hair with sticky marshmallow covered hands OR melted chocolate covered hands?

Spend two hours going to the grocery store for carrots and then leaving a carrot trail around your house for the Easter Bunny OR three hours making homemade sugar cookies for Santa Claus's cookie plate?

Would You Rather...

Wear a pair of shoes made from plastic Easter eggs OR wear socks made from cotton balls?

Go on an Easter egg hunt at your school playground with all the rest of the kids at your school at the same time OR go on an Easter egg hunt where you compete alongside kids and adults to find the most eggs?

Would You Rather...

Find your Easter basket stuck in a big gooey mud puddle OR frozen into a yellow snowbank?

Get a different colored Easter basket every year with different candies in it OR get the same exact colored Easter basket with the same exact amount and kind of candies in it?

Would You Rather...

Be covered in the pretty, soft yellow fluff of a little chick OR have the long floppy ears of a bunny rabbit?

Make windchimes out of used forks and spoons from your school's cafeteria OR make a windchime out of eggshells painted with metallic paint?

Would You Rather...

Be able to hop leaps and bounds everywhere you go like a bunny OR have a cute little fluffy white tail coming out of your behind like a bunny?

Compete in a swinging contest with your teacher at recess, the winner gets an Easter egg OR at a park after school with your mom or dad?

Would You Rather...

Everything you eat for the month of April taste like coconut OR everything you smell for the month of April smell like a beachy fresh bottle of coconut sunscreen?

End every sentence by saying "That's egg-citing!" OR begin every sentence with "I'm hoppy to report"?

Would You Rather...

Be able to jump over cars and playground equipment like a giant Easter bunny OR be able to squeeze through tiny spaces like cracks in a fence like a tiny Easter chick?

Throw an Easter party with a bunch of hip-hoppy bunny rabbits OR with a bunch of chirpy techno baby chickens?

Would You Rather...

Have a basket of beautifully decorated Easter eggs that smell rotten OR a bunch of really ugly duckling decorated Easter eggs that are filled with chocolate?

Spend an afternoon picking fragrant daisies at a flower garden OR mowing yards for people in your neighborhood?

Would You Rather...

Spend an afternoon hanging colored plastic
Easter eggs on trees in your front yard
OR spend your afternoon hiding a bunch
of dyed hard-boiled eggs all around
your yard?

Put on a puppet show by coloring your
fingers with Easter egg dye OR creating
finger puppets out of painted eggshells?

Would You Rather...

Get an Easter basket filled with wet spaghetti instead of grass OR an Easter basket filled with year-old rock-hard marshmallow bunnies?

Bite into a marshmallow chick that was left over from last Easter OR eat a chocolate bunny that someone else took a big bite out of?

Would You Rather...

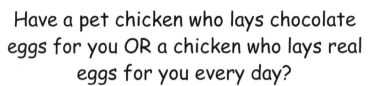

Have a pet chicken who lays chocolate eggs for you OR a chicken who lays real eggs for you every day?

Spend the day after Easter at the dentist's office because of all the sugar you ate on Easter OR spend the day after the 4th of July at the ear doctor because you were sitting too close to the fireworks show?

Would You Rather...

Drink a big glass of water that is clear but tastes like chocolate OR eat a big chocolate bunny that looks and smells delicious but like water has no taste?

Eat a piece of toast covered with shaved coconut OR get an edible Easter basket made from chocolate?

 Would You Rather...

Wear a big fancy flower-covered Easter hat that attracts bees to your head OR one covered in chocolate eggs which melt in the sun and drip into your eyes?

Dress up as a neon green Easter bunny and not get recognized as the Easter bunny OR dress up as a fuzzy little hot pink chick?

Would You Rather...

Swim in a giant pool filled with fruity flavored little jellybeans OR in a hot tub filled with melted chocolate bunnies?

Have a jumbo cotton ball stapled to your rear end like a rabbit's tail OR stick a chewed-on piece of pink bubble gum to the tip of your nose like a bunny nose?

Would You Rather...

Wear a headband with floppy Easter bunny ears OR wear a big fluffy Easter Bunny cotton tail to school for a whole day?

Go to see your favorite baseball team play a game on opening day of baseball season OR go to the swimming pool on the opening day of summer swimming?

Would You Rather...

Run around the park trying to catch butterflies with a net OR trying to catch tadpoles with your bare hands on a beautiful spring day?

Spend an afternoon feeding smelly ducks at the pond OR spend an afternoon digging acorns for the twitchy squirrels at the park?

Would You Rather...

Be able to shoot plastic eggs out of your mouth OR jellybeans out of your belly button on command?

Make a handprint flower out of construction paper and accidentally cut off your paper pinkie finger OR let out a big juicy sneeze all over your paper flower?

Would You Rather...

Celebrate the first day of spring by flying a kite on a day with barely a breeze OR by jumping in puddles and getting mud all up the back of your clothes and in your shoes?

Spill your bottle of bubbles before you can even blow one bubble OR get a hole in your kite before you can send it up in the air?

 # Would You Rather...

Have speckled blue eyes like a robin's egg OR fluffy blond hair like a small chick?

Spill a glass of orange juice on your Easter Sunday best clothing OR get a marshmallow rabbit squished under the seat of your pants or dress?

Would You Rather...

Try to climb to the top of a tree that doesn't have its leaves yet OR try to climb to the top of a tree that is thickly covered with leaves?

Find your Easter basket on Easter morning and find eggs made from chalk in it OR eggs made from clay in the basket?

Would You Rather...

Have a pet lamb who follows you to school every day and sits beside your desk OR have a pet rock who you drag along by a leash wherever you go?

Glue together a life-sized lamb out of cotton balls OR make a blanket to snuggle under by gluing together tissues from an entire box of Kleenex?

Would You Rather...

Paint all your Easter eggs with cups of paint and a paintbrush instead of dipping them into cups of dye OR shoot paintballs at your Easter eggs from across the yard?

Start summer break the day after Easter OR end summer break the day after the 4th of July?

Would You Rather...

Stick two boiled Easter eggs in your mouth at the same time OR stuff a whole package of marshmallow rabbits in your mouth at the same time?

Try to skip a bunch of thick, round stones across a pond OR try to build a sandcastle with sand that's bone dry?

Would You Rather...

Take a walk outside on a cloudy and rainy day without an umbrella or raincoat OR spend an afternoon out in the bright sunshine without any sunscreen?

Wash your hair with fruity jellybean scented shampoo OR brush your teeth with licorice flavored toothpaste?

Would You Rather...

Get rained on during the middle of your spring picnic OR drop your sandwich into a mud puddle during the picnic?

Go to school on Easter if you could have a longer spring break OR have your school's spring break be part of your Easter holiday break?

Would You Rather...

Have a caterpillar crawl up the sleeve of your shirt OR a butterfly become tangled in your hair?

Grow whiskers overnight that grow back every time you shave them off OR walk around school every day making bunny ears on everyone you're near?

Would You Rather...

Eat chocolate candy that makes your lips, teeth, and tongue turn black OR eat jellybeans that turn your lips, teeth, and tongue green?

Pay a quarter for each piece of chocolate you eat on Easter morning OR get paid a quarter for each piece of chocolate you eat on Easter morning?

Would You Rather...

Celebrate Easter in the middle of summer where your chocolate eggs turn into little brown puddles OR celebrate Easter in the middle of winter where your chocolate eggs are frozen like little brown ice cubes?

Get tangled up in your kite's string and fall on the ground OR get hit in the leg by a jump rope end that came loose from your hand?

 Would You Rather...

Have brown melted chocolate stuck underneath your fingernails OR have a bunch of brown dirt stuck underneath your fingernails?

See who can roll an Easter egg the farthest down a sidewalk OR see who can bounce a marshmallow chick the highest off the floor?

104

Would You Rather...

Dip your bare toes in a green slimy looking pond OR dig your bare hands deep into a squishy brown mud puddle?

Go on a field trip to the museum and get lost in the dinosaur display OR a field trip to the library and get lost in a favorite Easter book?

Would You Rather...

Get sticky marshmallow creme on the screen of your phone OR stuck in the keys of your computer keyboard?

Collect your family's used toilet paper tubes OR discarded dirty eggshells to plant vegetable seedlings in for your class garden?

Would You Rather...

Play a game of soccer by kicking around
an extra large Easter egg OR play a game
of golf by hitting Easter eggs around
the course?

Celebrate Easter with the Easter Toad
instead of the Easter Bunny OR be visited
by Belsnickel on Christmas Eve instead
of Santa Claus?

Did you enjoy the book?

If you did, we are eggs-static. If not, please write your complaint to us and we will ensure we fix it.

If you're feeling generous, there is something important that you can help me with - tell other people that you enjoyed the book.

Ask a grown-up to write about it on Amazon. When they do, more people will find out about the book. It also lets Amazon know that we are making kids around the world laugh. Even a few words and ratings would go a long way.

If you have any ideas or jokes that you think are super funny, please let us know. We would love to hear from you. Our email address is - **riddleland@riddlelandforkids.com**

Riddleland Bonus Book

Join our **Facebook Group**
at **Riddleland for Kids** to get
daily jokes and riddles.

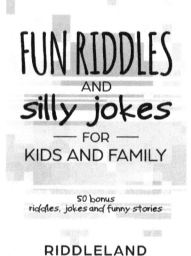

http://pixelfy.me/riddlelandbonus

Thank you for buying this book. We would like to share a special bonus as a token of appreciation. It is a collection of 50 original jokes, riddles, and two super funny stories.

Would you like your jokes and riddles to be featured in our next book?

We are having a contest to see who are the smartest or funniest boys and girls in the world! :

1) Creative and Challenging Riddles

2) Tickle Your Funny Bone Contest

Parents, please email us your child's "original" Riddle or Joke and **he or she could win a $25 Amazon gift card and be featured in our next book.**

Here are the rules:

1) We're looking for super challenging riddles and extra funny jokes.

2) Jokes and riddles MUST be 100% original—NOT something discovered on the Internet.

3) You can submit both a joke and a riddle because they are two separate contests.

4) Don't get help from your parents—unless they're as funny as you are.

5) Winners will be announced via email or our Facebook group – Riddleland for Kids

6) In your entry, please confirm which book you purchased.

7) Email us at Riddleland@riddlelandforkids.com

Other Fun Children Books for Kids!

Riddles Series

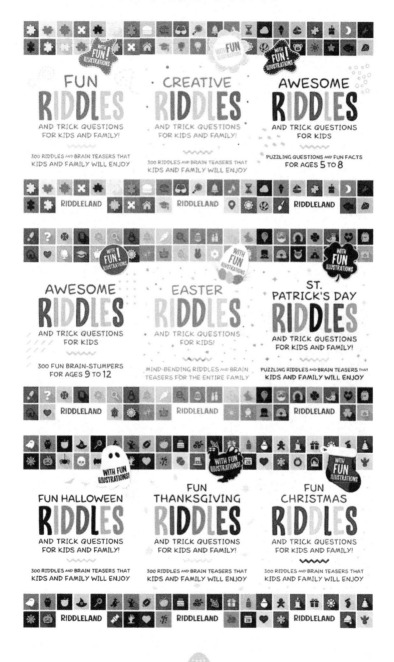

The Laugh Challenge Joke Series

Would You Rather... Series

About Riddleland

Riddleland is a mom + dad run publishing company. We are passionate about creating fun and innovative books to help children develop their reading skills and fall in love with reading. If you have suggestions for us or want to work with us, shoot us an email at riddleland@riddlelandforkids.com

Check out our website at www.riddlelandforkids.com

Our family's favorite quote:

"Creativity is an area in which younger people have a tremendous advantage since they have an endearing habit of always questioning past wisdom and authority."
~ Bill Hewlett

Made in the USA
Las Vegas, NV
28 March 2021